Carolina Shag
The Spirit of Southern Social Dance

~

An Introduction to the Timeless Tradition of Shag Dancing in the Carolinas

Table of Contents

Page

7   Dedication

13   Chapter One
         - History and Culture of the Carolina Shag

25   Chapter Two
         - Shag Culture Today

45   Chapter Three
         - Beach Music and Counting Dance Steps

47   Chapter Four
         - Social Dance

49   Chapter Five
         - Shag Dance Introductory Lessons

67   Shag Term Glossary

73   Acknowledgments

76   Life on the Dance Floor

Dedication

This book is dedicated to my mentors and teachers in dance,
especially the
very fine dancing ladies

the late Caroline Thode Ballenger,
Joyce Ballenger Rush and Loucinda Brewer Price,
and the late Betty Brady Stockman

who gave me
this wonderful life as a dancer

Dear Readers,

Being raised in upstate South Carolina, my first awareness of the Shag was during family gatherings at my aunt's house, when adults would disappear into her dance studio in the backyard and play records that I noticed had a strange and alluring beat. I watched my aunt and her friends grin enormously as they obviously enjoyed this dance that they called "Shaggin," and told me I was entirely too young to do it. Of course, that made me immediately determined to learn.

My older cousins visited a magical place they called Ocean Drive, and I hoped eagerly to be able to go there someday.

By the time I arrived in Columbia to attend the University of South Carolina at age 17, I knew Shag steps and had of course spent time at Myrtle Beach (if you grow up in South Carolina, this is a given), but my real introduction to Shag culture came after I wandered down that brick alley in 5 Points and walked through the door of *Pug's*. There, I was exposed to the diversity of Shag styles from around South Carolina and was highly encouraged to make frequent visits to Ocean Drive, which we quite often did, even if only for the evening.

As I had grown up dancing and training in a variety of dance genres, nothing pleased me more than to have an opportunity to actually be paid to teach others how to dance. Imagine my joy, that same year, at hearing that *Beau's* in the Carolina Inn was looking for someone to teach Shag during happy hour...as a fun activity to warm up the crowd for the real Shag lessons, taught by Mitch Barkoot and Jo-Jo Putnam later in the evening. I was their warm-up act. What a job.

I always credit the experience of leading inebriated adults in a dance activity with preparing me to teach social dance to elementary-age children.

In my career as a dancer, the joy of dancing the Carolina Shag has never worn off for me.

As I sit finishing this book on the second floor of a pleasantly shabby beach house on First Avenue, Ocean Drive, I am gazing at the view of the ocean over the Pavilion and waiting for the afternoon sun to tell me it is time to walk down the street for yet another Shag social, to dance with friends of many years as well as meet new friends and dance partners.

Enjoy reading…and then get out there and join the fun for the rest of your life! See you on the dance floor…

Miss Caroline

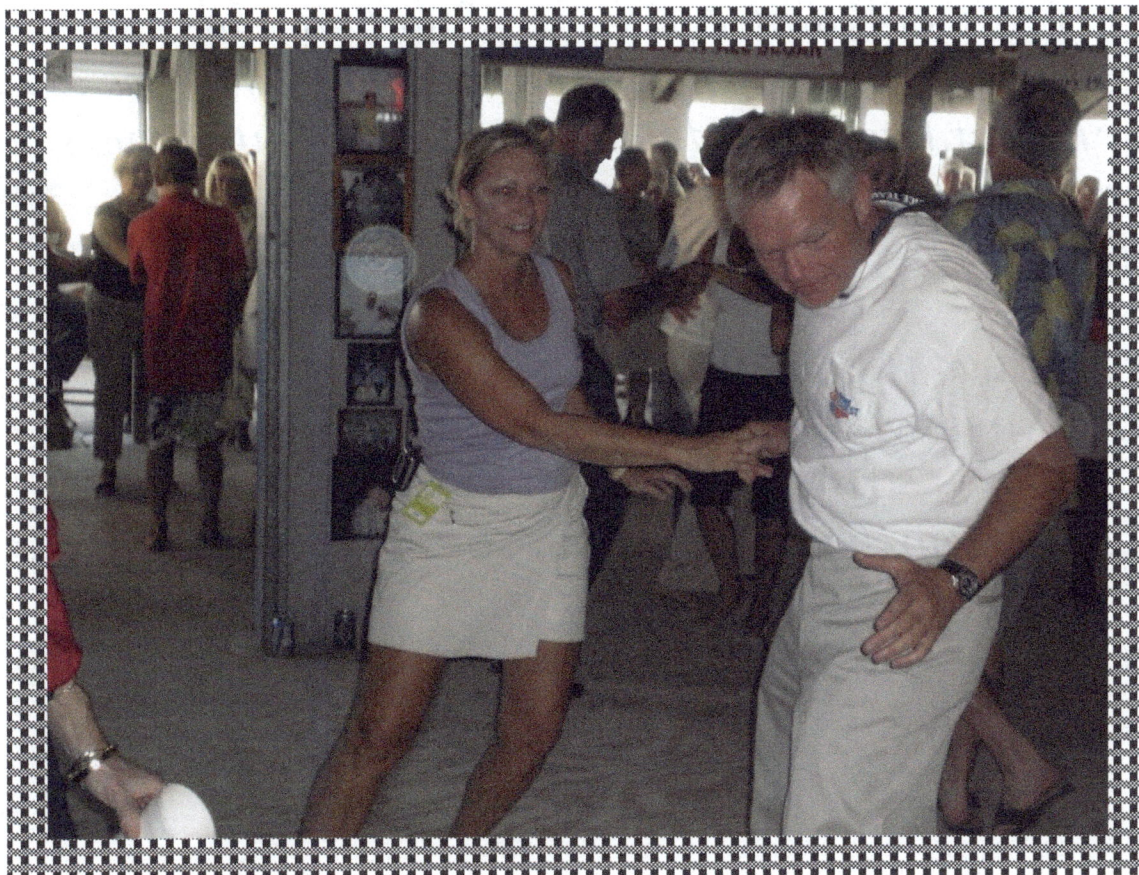

Caroline Hoadley and longtime North Carolina Shagger Randall Long Shaggin' at the Ocean Drive Pavilion in North Myrtle Beach, SC.

Summers at the beach, cruising on the boulevard, boys and girls, leather soles sliding on sanded wood, the rhythms of the waves and the blues...

The Carolina Shag has spanned generations, and remains an integral part of Southern culture today, as one of the threads in the madras that is the South.

A true social dance, the Carolina Shag has regional and generational differences in steps and style but has unified generations of Southerners with its improvisational nature, social atmosphere, and soulful magic.

Come feel the rhythms, slide your feet...follow...lead...who will you meet?

Learn your basic, try it out and see, but darlin'...

Save the Last Dance for Me...

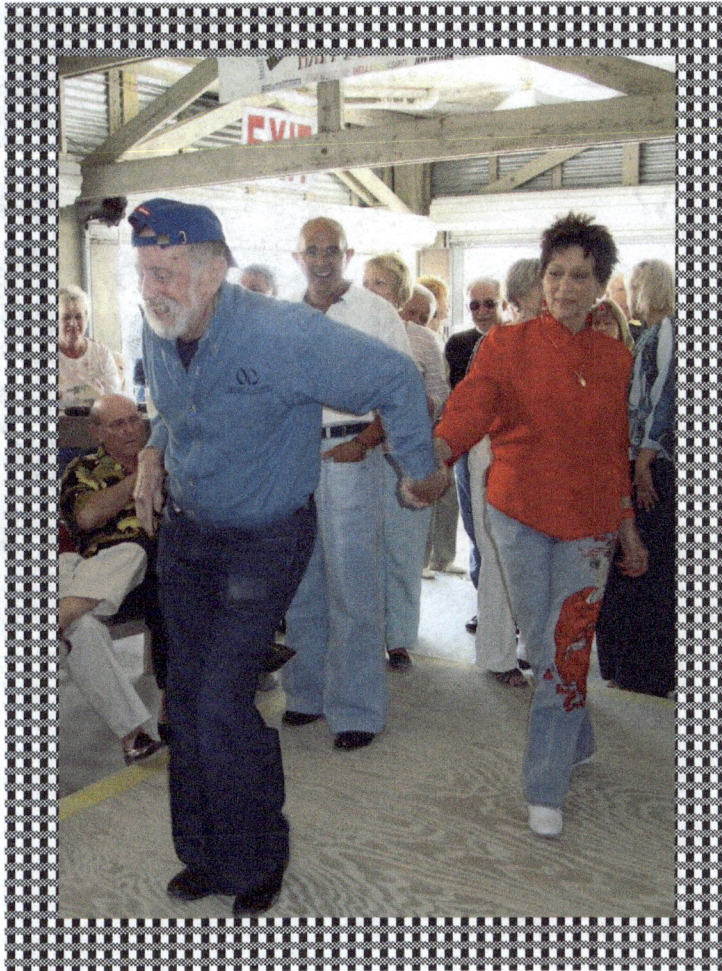

"It's controlled wildness...a self-expression without being vulgar, just tasty enough to let you know what's happening."

"You dance to that beat, and the beat has a pulse, just like your heart. And you get into rhythmic values, coordinating with the beat of the music, so you're playing right along with the musicians. You're improvising. Improv...that's where your self-expression comes out"

- Jo-Jo Putnam, member of the Shag Hall of Fame
and a dancing free spirit

Joanne Johnson (above) shags with Jo-Jo in the OD Pavilion at SOS.

Ellen Taylor and
Jo-Jo Putnam
grace the water
tower at
Ocean Drive

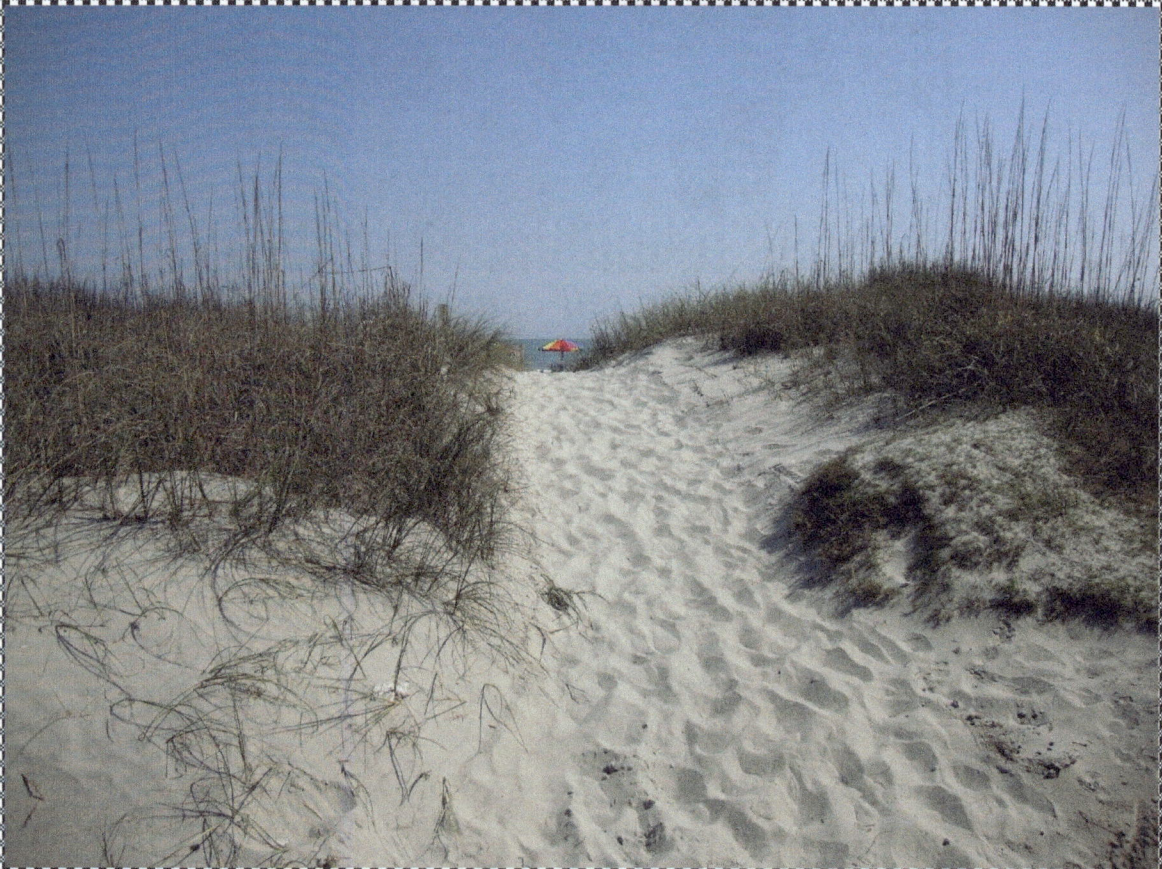

Chapter One
History and Culture of the Carolina Shag

What is the Shag?

The Carolina Shag is a social dance that began to evolve along the coast of the Carolinas during World War II, took shape in the 1940s, and came of age in the 1950s continuing as an integral part of southern culture to this very day. Originally called "fast dance", "boogie", "jitterbugging" and "jukin", the name "Shag" was not applied to this dance until the second half of the twentieth century but is now used to define the genre.

A member of the swing dance family, the Shag is different from other members of that family; it does not hop and jump…it is characterized by smooth sliding steps executed low to the floor.

Since its beginning and to this day, the Shag has been an integral part of Southern culture. From the beach to cities, towns, and lakeside resorts across the Carolinas, Shag dance and Beach music have been a uniquely Southern social vehicle and rite of passage for the young in the South. The most interesting aspect of the dance is the improvisational nature of the Shag. Improvisation actually defines the Shag as a social dance.

Each dancer improvises movements within the structure of the basic and never knows exactly what the other will be doing.

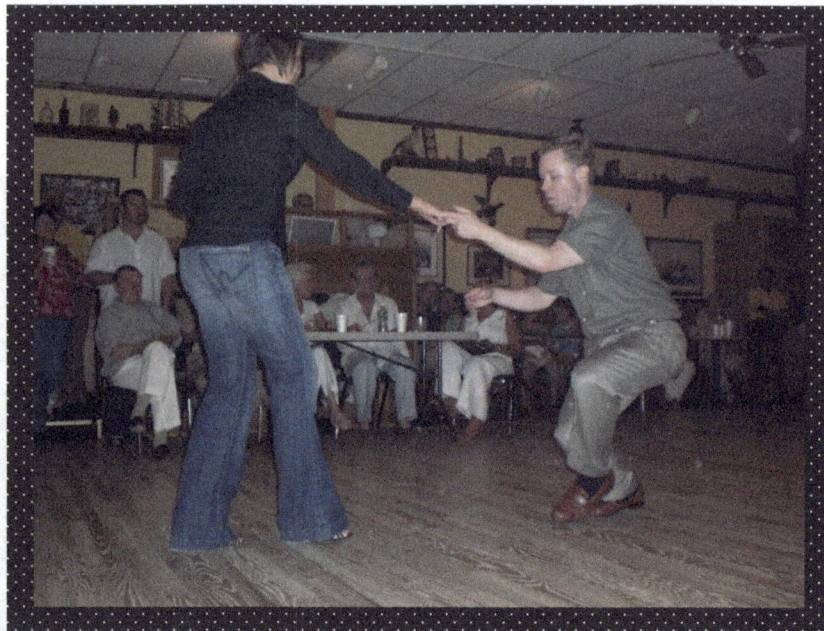

As in ballroom dances, the Gentleman leads and Lady follows. Unlike swing or ballroom dances, it is the man who shows off more intricate steps as the lady keeps the beat and the slotted pathway intact while improvising her steps within that structure.

Evolution of the Carolina Shag in Dance History

All dances evolve from other dances over time, while being affected by multiple influences. Shag is no exception.

American swing and jazz dance began with immigrants from different cultures in the port cities of the south playing music and dancing in close proximity to each other, thereby combining the arts of their cultures and creating a new American art form.

The first dance to come of this collaboration was the Charleston, a lively 8-count ragtime dance that evolved in the early 20th century. The Charleston steps, danced to 4/4 musical time and counted in 8 musical beats, come from a mixture of West African dance, Irish dance, and European peasant folk dance. The Charleston moves in a "slotted" pattern, dancers holding hands as they travel forward and backward, toward and away from their partners.

The next swing dance during the 1920s was the Lindy Hop, which appeared as the Charleston basic was turned sideways, partners still holding hands. Dancers needed a sideways motion to execute their acrobatic partner work. (A variation of the Charleston called the Collegiate Shag but with little similarity to the Carolina Shag, incorporated hopping and leaping steps and was popular for a short period during this time.)

As swing dance became even more mainstream in the 1930s, the 6-count Swing basic swept across the country. This basic was the Lindy basic without 2 of the counts. Americans were used to dancing in the ballroom position, which prohibited the last 2 counts of the Lindy from being comfortably executed, so those counts were left out, leaving only 6 musical beats. The Swing was danced in the ballroom position moving sideways, with a quarter turn on the rock step.

Swing dancers began to call themselves Jitterbugs. During the 1940s in the North, Jitterbugs then began to sometimes revert back to the 8-count basic, adding 2 counts at the end of the 6, and opened up the closed ballroom position, returning to the holding of both hands. In the South, along the Carolina coast, Jitterbugs kept the 6 counts, opened up the closed basic, and began to move in the old, slotted pattern, toward and away from their partner in the Charleston style, utilizing the holding of only one hand in order to better facilitate improvisation.

The Big Apple and Little Apple, dances from Columbia in 1936 which became national dance crazes, heavily influenced the technique, style, and improvisational footwork of the southern jitterbugs. The Big Apple is a circle dance that includes most of the popular steps of the 1920s and 1930s. Circle dances are seen around the world, and have different aspects from partner or line dances. A caller led the Big Apple, and dancers improvised steps based on the calls. Dancers moving to the middle of the circle and executing the footwork as a couple became the "Little Apple". "Truckin' on down", "Posin" and Suzi-Q" are a just a few of the Big Apple/Little Apple steps that influenced Shaggers' footwork and style.

As the improvisational nature of Shag dance grew, dancers began to hold only one of their partner's hands, in the style of The Little Apple, rather than hold both hands in order to improvise more freely. Dancers began to keep their feet closer to the floor, sliding rather than stepping, and a new style became a new dance…the Shag.

Since the beginning of ragtime/jazz and the Charleston, both black and white communities in the South had danced and enjoyed jazz music and dance. Although segregation was the rule and law during the early 20th century, throughout history it is the nature of musicians and dancers, especially the young, to interact and share art with others. Late at night in clubs and juke joints or in private venues, black and white musicians and dancers interacted and the evolution of the music and dance spread through both communities, especially through the young adults.

In the 1940s young white dancers became aware of emerging music called the blues, played by black musicians and therefore legally unavailable to the average white teen or young adult. Along the coast, which was less populated and less regulated at the time, the young devised ways to access the music, and any juke joint that played this forbidden music was assured of a large crowd of young dancers.

For this reason, Rhythm and Blues (R&B) music was first heard by white youth of the Carolinas at the beach and came to be referred to as "that music we hear at the beach" or "Beach music".

Then, as today, southerners gravitated toward the coast in the summertime, and many Southern family vacations were at the beach. In the south, summers at the beach and social activities there created lifelong friendships and connections that kept dancers returning to the coastal culture, especially the young. Partly due to military tactics (blackouts and whiteouts) on the Carolina coast during WWII, and also due to the geographical layout of the coastline, the gathering places at the beaches for the young dancers spanned from Wilmington, NC's Carolina Beach to Charleston, SC's Folly Beach.

The central hub of dancing activity became known as the long coastal crescent in South Carolina called the "Grand Strand", the center of which is Myrtle Beach, since there was a large number of pavilions and juke joints in close proximity to one another there.

The Ocean Drive Pavilion sits on the site of
the old Roberts Pavilion

at Ocean Drive Beach, North Myrtle Beach, SC.

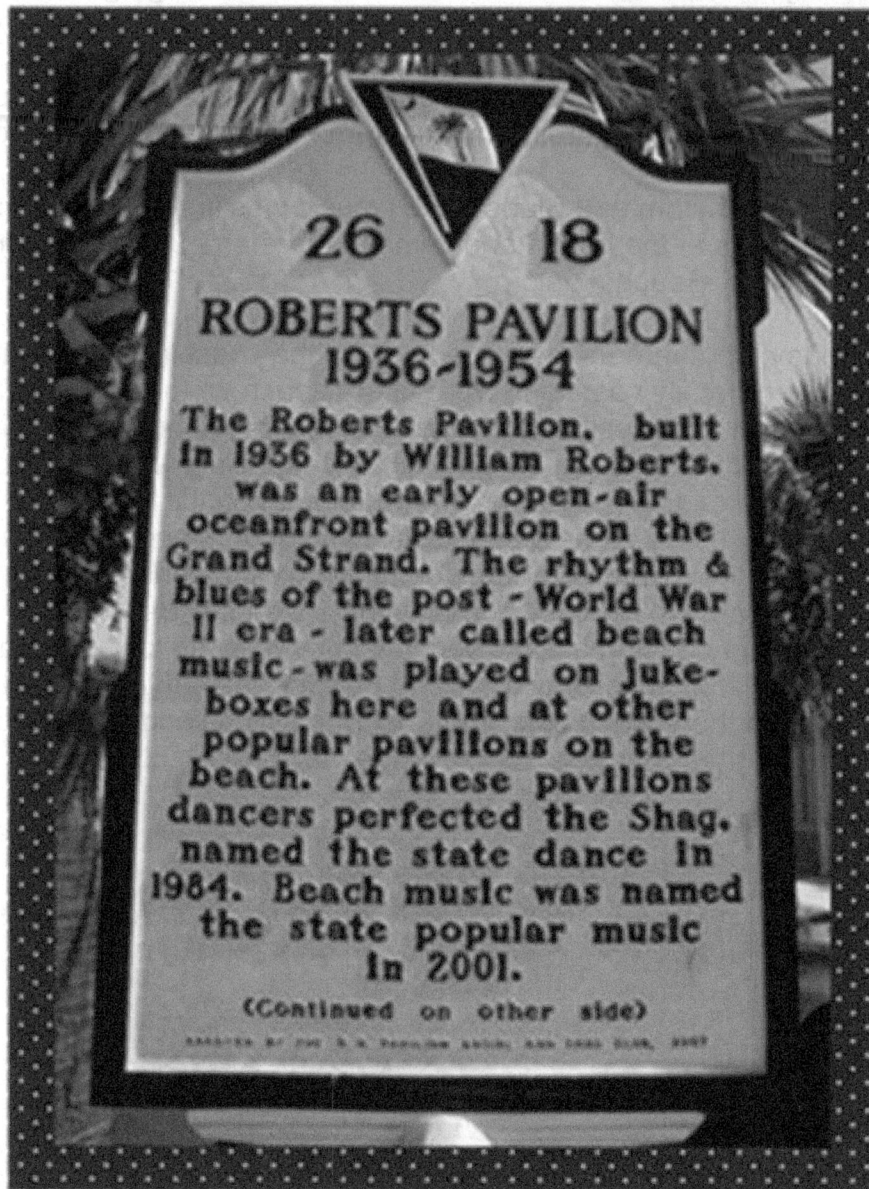

26   18

ROBERTS PAVILION
1936-1954

The Roberts Pavilion, built in 1936 by William Roberts, was an early open-air oceanfront pavilion on the Grand Strand. The rhythm & blues of the post-World War II era - later called beach music - was played on jukeboxes here and at other popular pavilions on the beach. At these pavilions dancers perfected the Shag, named the state dance in 1984. Beach music was named the state popular music in 2001.

(Continued on other side)

The Roberts Pavilion was partially destroyed by Hurricane Hazel in 1954. Parts of the old Roberts Pavilion are intact in the reconstructed Ocean Drive Pavilion, rebuilt between 1955-57

In 2009, this historical marker was placed at the site of the old Sonny's Pavilion at Cherry Grove Beach, SC where young Shaggers convened late at night after the North Myrtle Beach curfew sent them north to dance until the wee hours before dawn...

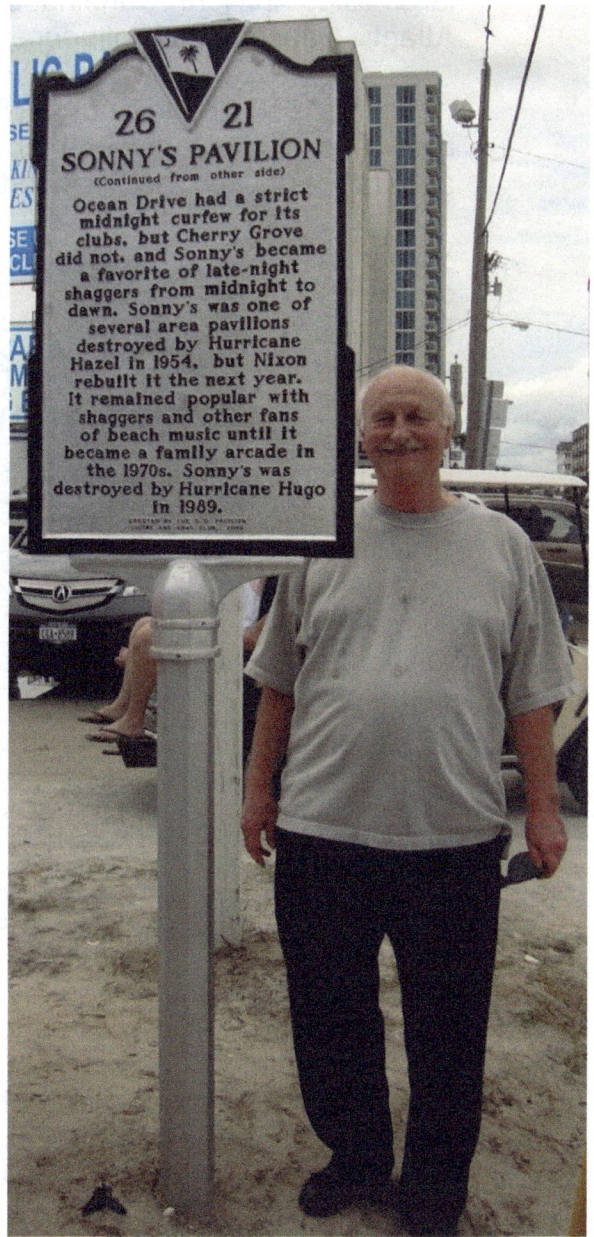

Just north of Myrtle Beach there was a black beach, Atlantic Beach, which still exists today. The close juxtaposition of R&B music and black performers and dancers in the nightclubs there to the neighboring white beaches facilitated intercultural influence between all the dancing youth to the immediate south in Myrtle Beach and the immediate north in Ocean Drive Beach as well as in Atlantic Beach itself.

Atlantic Beach, being halfway between New York and Miami, was a friendly stopping and performance point for blues performers on their way between the large cities. In North Carolina, the dance style varied, as it was farther away from Atlantic Beach and its influence.

In the 1950s in the South, R&B or Beach music replaced Swing as the musical choice of the young, and the meshing of black and white styles in music and dance defined the Shag further, making it unique as a social dance.

Young dancers traveled up and down the coast, intermingling at North and South Carolina beaches as well as taking the dance steps home with them inland, where Shag styles further evolved and varied throughout  the rest of the twentieth century and to the present day. Shag dance has survived through many musical and dance eras and has remained a cultural constant in southern culture.

In 1984, Representative "Bubber" Snow of Hemmingway, SC proposed legislation making Shag the official state dance of South Carolina. In 2001, Beach music became the official state music of South Carolina. North Carolina, in 2005, designated Shag as its official state dance as well.

During the pandemic of the early 2020s, socializing suddenly came to a screeching halt, with clubs canceling events and dancers staying home. A decision was even made to cancel SOS in an effort to keep illnesses at a minimum.

Many iconic Shaggers passed away during this unprecedented time.

The beach was silent and still, as all waited for the time to pass...

Thankfully, and by the Grace of God, the dawn of a new season!

Photo by Monty Lee

*Shaggers emerged once again on the dance floors, and
music fills the air…*

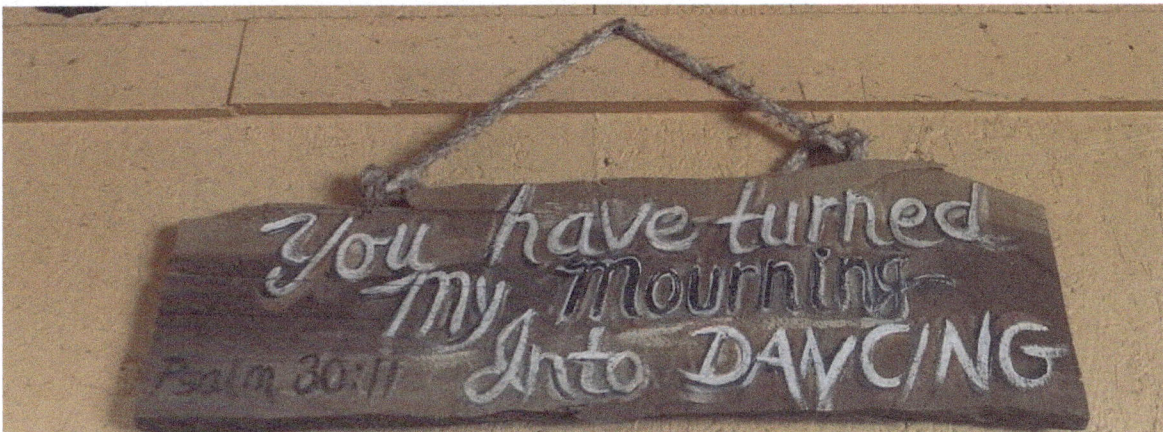

23

Chapter 2 - Shag Culture Today

Today, Ocean Drive Beach in North Myrtle Beach is the Home of the Shag.

The Shag Hall of Fame is there, with pictures and stories displayed in the Ocean Drive Resort.

Names of famous Shaggers are embedded in the sidewalk in a Walk of Fame on Main Street.

In the hallways of the OD Resort, pictures and stories of Hall of Famers tell the stories of the Beach dancing icons and are a living history of 20th century Beach culture.

The "**Keepers of the Dance**" is a hall of fame of the best young Shaggers, the next generation of Shag culture. Keepers are enshrined in photos and memorabilia in Fat Harolds Dance Club on Main Street, Ocean Drive Beach.

The OD Pavilion, in the horseshoe at the end of Main Street, has weathered many hurricanes and floods over nearly a century and welcomes old and new Shaggers to its dance floor in season.

Although the Pavilion is the historical centerpiece of Ocean Drive Beach, other clubs such as Fat Harolds, Ducks, HOTOs, The Spanish Galleon, The OD Arcade, Pirates Cove, and others are filled with music and dancing

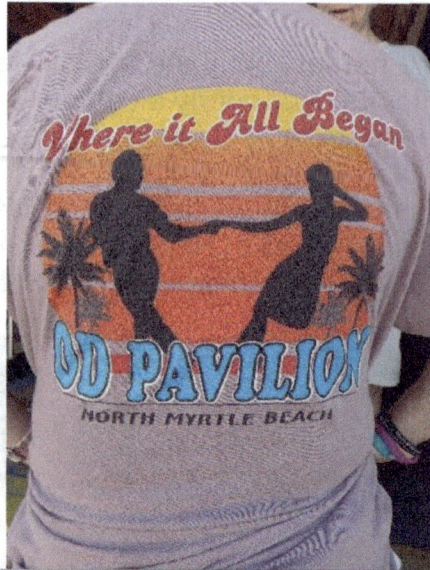

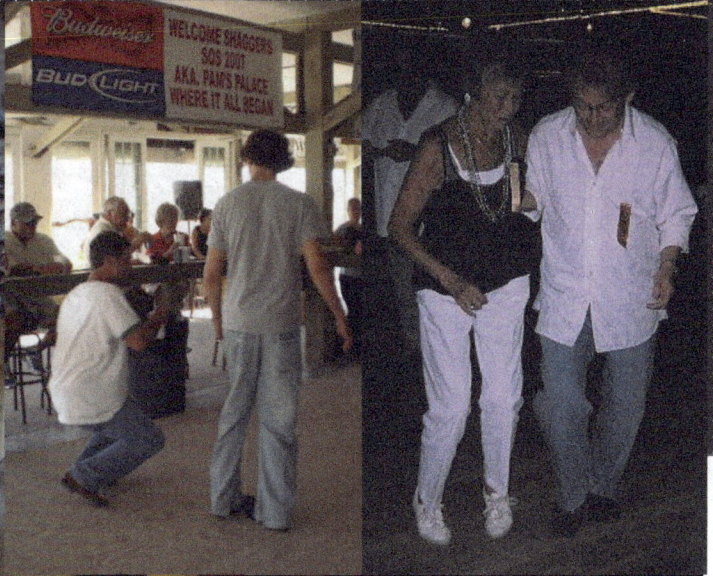

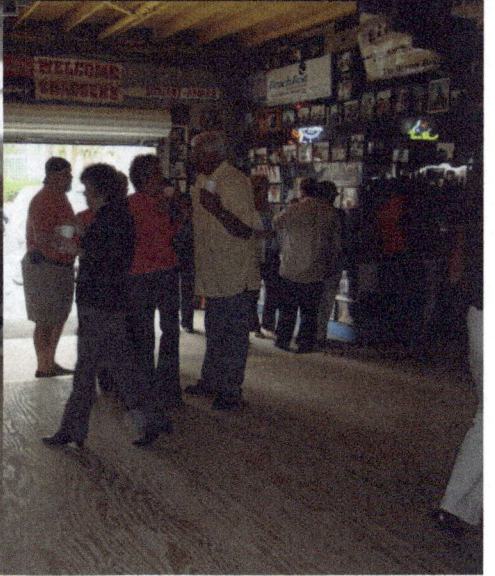

Fat Harolds

FAT HAROLD'S BEACH CLUB

The Ocean Drive Resort's

Spanish Galleon

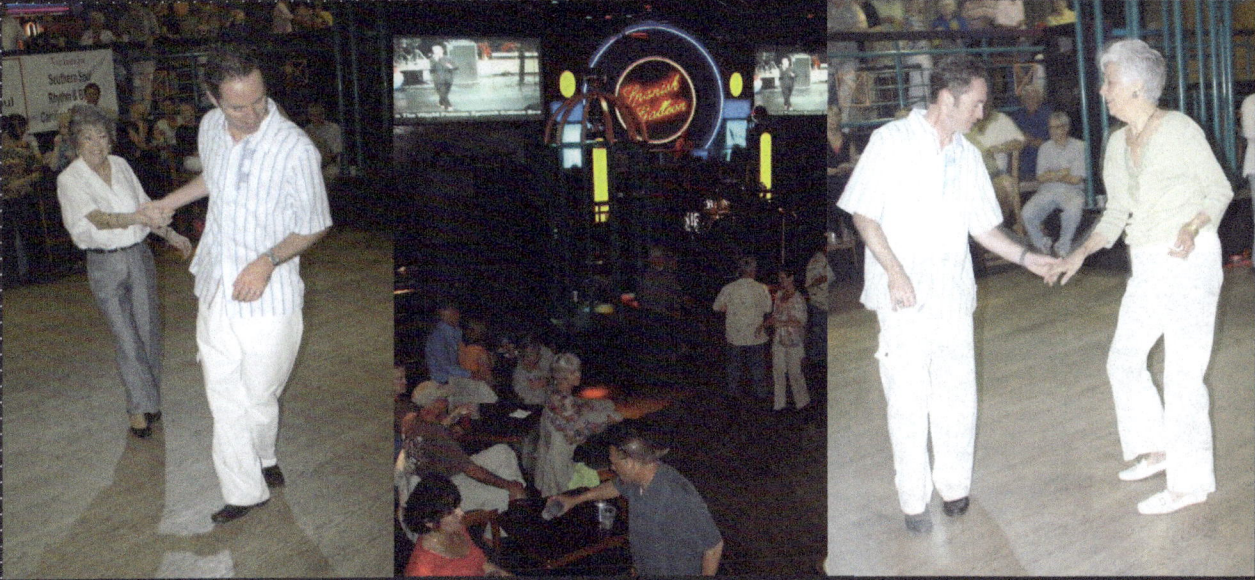

And HOTO's

The Arcade
Lounge

Pirate's Cove

And others

There are numerous Shag Social Clubs across the Carolinas and throughout the nation. Most social clubs are under the umbrella of the ACSC, or Association of Carolina Shag Clubs, founded in 1984. Competitive Shagging exists with both professional and amateur contests nationally for both adults and juniors. The ACSC sponsors contests that lead to the National Championships, and there are also independent contests for partners as well as mixed-doubles contests.

The Society of Stranders (SOS) began in 1980 as a reunion gathering of lifeguards and those who had lived and worked at the beach, and now SOS hosts three adult gatherings yearly at Ocean Drive for those who come from across the nation to dance, hear Beach Music, and see the best Shag dancers. Fall Migration, Mid-Winter SOS, and Spring Safari bring thousands to dance at OD. In the summer during JR.SOS, aspiring young dancers are able to dance on the famous floors.

SOS Good Friends, Good Times, Great Memories

Junior SOS is held every July, and dancers aged 3 to 20 take over Ocean Drive with social dancing, dance classes, parties, and dance contests. Keepers of the Dance is a rite of passage for Junior Shaggers, as every year Keepers are chosen from those aging out of juniors when they reach 21 years of age.

Celebrating the Shag becoming South Carolina's State Dance and the formation of the Association of Carolina Shag Clubs!

Shag Dance Steps and Style

Dancers in different parts of the South vary their Shag steps and style. Some words used to reference different styles are "smooth" or "smoothie", "boogie" and "bop". Different ages or generations have had slightly different styles as the Shag has evolved through the decades. In that way, it is very much like a folk dance, evolving regionally around a particular pattern.

There are many accepted "Basics", as the main step in any social dance is called. Some other dances look similar, but in order to be the Shag, several things need to be in place:

Dancers must be moving in a slotted pattern on the basic moving toward and away from their partner, holding only one hand.

Dancers must be completing a basic on 6 musical counts.

Dancers' steps in the basic are low to the floor, sliding smoothly.

Dance partners may execute steps in sync with each other, but they also use improvisation and may improvise most of the dance within the criteria above.

In Shag dance, there is a smooth continuity and flow in the footwork as dancers execute steps and improvisations.

Many famous dancers from South and North Carolina who have been instrumental in defining Shag dance are depicted in the Shag Hall of Fame at the OD Resort hallways, on various websites, in books on the Shag, and in SOS publications.

Chapter Three
Beach Music and Counting Dance steps

Musical beats

The reason dancers count dance in numbers is to keep in time with the music. Dance is counted on musical beats, and music has been counted, and written in a universal manner, all over the world consistently for at least 500 years.

The wor "beat" denotes the downbeat of the music, a constant beat. The word "count" means to count those beats. The beats are counted in numbers.
Musical time is denoted by how many beats are in a measure, and how many beats are assigned to the "quarter notes". For instance, 4/4 Musical time means that there are 4 beats in a measure, and the quarter note (4) gets one beat.
So, in 4/4 musical time, one measure of downbeats would be counted "**1 2 3 4**".

Additional beats between the downbeats create a Rhythm.
Between each downbeat is the "upbeat"
Any movement executed on the upbeat is counted by the word "**AND**", not by adding another downbeat or number, as the downbeat pattern must stay consistent with the musical time.

Many dances (but not all) are performed to music in 4/4 musical time. This means one measure has 4 beats. Dancers traditionally count a step in 2 measures, as 4 beats is not a very long time to execute a step. Therefore, around the world, dancers are usually counting in 8s.

The Shag is danced to Carolina Beach Music, which is in 4/4 musical time, but the basic is completed in 6 musical counts rather than 8. That means the Shag basic takes one and one-half measures, the next basic will start in the middle of a measure, and it will not be until the third measure that the first count of the basic will be on the first count of a measure.

Carolina Beach Music

"Beach Music" is the term commonly used in the South to refer to R&B (rhythm and blues) music that was the popular music on the South Carolina coast, was instrumental in the evolution of the Shag, and continues to be popular today. Originally called "race music" because it was primarily music by black artists, the music was embraced especially by the young. Although the music began to be widely popular with youth in the 1940s and 50s, the term "Beach Music" did not become common until the 1960s, and did not become widespread in use until the 1970s.

One reason the phrase "Beach Music" was coined was that "race music" was legally not played on mainstream white radio, and the only place young people were able to experience the music was on the jukeboxes at the Pavilions of the Carolina coastline and its juke joints, in other words, at the Beach. In 2001 Beach music was designated as the official state music in South Carolina.

This music has continued to be popular in the South and now, both old and new bands and songs keep Beach Music alive in the heartbeat of Southern culture. Not all Beach Music songs are danceable, but most are.

Some good songs for beginners, especially the young, for Shag dancing are:

"Carolina Girls" – General Johnson and the Chairmen of the Board
"Ocean Boulevard" – Band of Oz
"Ain't Nothin Like Shaggin" – The Tams
"Save the Last Dance for Me" – the Drifters
"Saturday Night at the Movies" – the Drifters
"Summertime's Calling Me" – the Catalinas
"I Love Beach Music" – the Embers

"Myrtle Beach Days" – the Fantastic Shakers
"Hey Hey Baby" – the Swingin' Medallions
"Beach Trip" - Billy Scott and the Prophets
"Talk That Talk" – Jackie Wilson
"Keep on Shaggin" – Calabash Flash
"One Drop of Love" — Ray Charles
"Hold on to the Blues" — Lonnie Givins
"Think" – The 5 Royales

Reginald Preston takes the mic, as Beach Music legends **The Mighty Tams** perform at Ducks
*"When you learn the Basic move, it adds something new…
let the music have control and twirl that girl around a time or two…"*
- Ain't Nothin' Like Shaggin' by the Tam

Chapter Four
Social Dance

Social Dances

All over the world for hundreds of years, people have danced to socialize and for fun and celebration. Knowledge of universal social dance manners and skills makes it possible for people to participate in this sort of activity at any age, wherever they are.
 Whether in a formal or casual setting, the basic rules are the same for all social dances:

* Gentlemen start on the Left foot, Ladies on the Right foot
* Gentlemen lead, and ladies follow
* At the end of each dance, both partners should look each other in the eye, shake hands, and thank each other verbally for the dance.
* Whether a Gentleman asks a lady to dance, or the Lady asks him, the Gentleman should lead the Lady to the dance floor by the hand and off the dance floor in the same manner.

The Carolina Shag is very much a social dance. In a social dance setting, people do not dance only with one partner or the person they came to the setting with. It is good manners to ask many people to dance, and this is how people socialize and meet others while dancing. In addition, leading and following skills are only obtained by dancing with as many different partners as possible. Traditionally, only the last dance of the evening is saved for someone special. In keeping with that tradition is the song by the Drifters, "Save the Last Dance for Me".

In Shag dance clubs in the south, this is understood by everyone, and it is not only permissible to ask strangers to dance, or accept if they ask you, it is considered good manners and friendly both to ask and to accept! If someone does not care to dance, they may say "I'm sorry, I am sitting this dance out" and there is no offense taken by either party.

Chapter Five
Shag Dance Introductory Lessons

Shag Progressions

Progressions are step-by-step lessons that build on the skills taught. The lessons in this book are designed to introduce Shag dance to the beginning non-dancer. This progression will facilitate success, and the ability of the student to participate in dancing with a partner quickly and easily.

The lessons are appropriate for ages 8 to adult, and after completing them, the next step would be to practice with as many different partners as possible and seek out more opportunities to learn, in order to move to the next level. There are MANY more basics, steps, and styles to learn about.

Lesson One
Dancing with a Partner and Social Skills

It is helpful for students to arrange themselves facing their partner, or if there are more than two students, in two lines facing each other (one for Ladies, one for Gentlemen) without holding hands.

Social skills learned in this lesson are not only for the Carolina Shag but for any social dance situation.

In asking someone to dance, there should be eye contact, a hand reaching out with the palm up (Left for Gentlemen, Right for Ladies), and the words "May I have this dance?" spoken clearly.

In accepting an offer, there should be eye contact, the corresponding hand (Left for Gentlemen, Right for Ladies) should be placed in the palm offered, and the words "Yes, you may" spoken clearly.

Sometimes Gentlemen ask Ladies to dance, and sometimes Ladies ask Gentlemen, but once there has been a request and an acceptance, it is the Gentleman's responsibility to lead the Lady to the dance floor and face his partner, holding her hands.

(In social dance lessons with unequal numbers of Ladies and Gentlemen, students without a partner should dance on their own practicing everything the students with partners are doing. In this way, their muscles will memorize the correct movements. It is NOT helpful for beginners of the same gender to dance with each other as their muscles will then memorize the wrong motions on the wrong foot.)

When dancing with a partner, Gentlemen are responsible for holding the Lady's hand. In the Shag, dancers hold only one hand (Lady's right, Gentlemen's Left.)

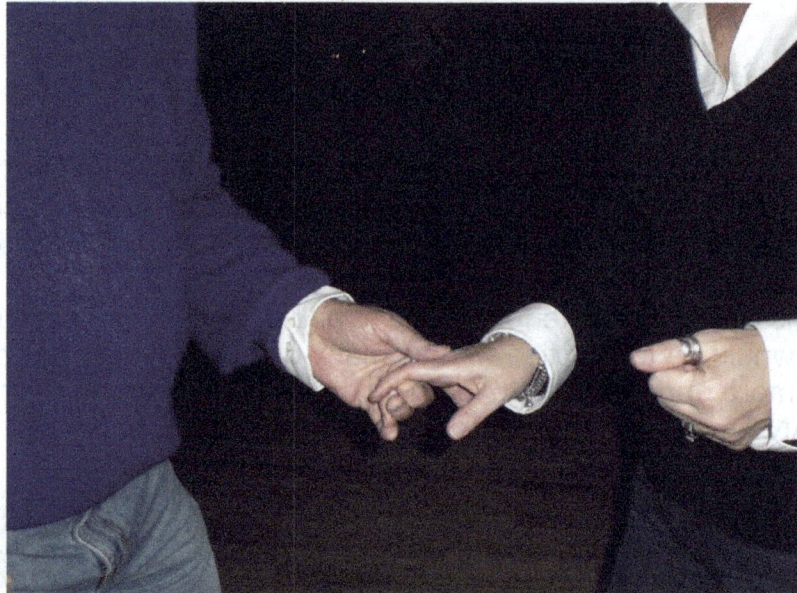

However, it is helpful for beginners to hold both hands, dropping the other hand only after dancers have become proficient at the basic. In this progression, wait until after completing Lesson 7 to drop the other hand.

All Shag basics are variations on the Walking Basic. The first Shag basic to learn is almost like walking, a constant weight shift from one foot to the other. Instead of stepping, the feet slide on the floor to change position on the first 4 counts. The feet do step rather than slide on the last 2 counts. As in all Shag basics, this basic is completed in 6 musical counts.

The **Leading** foot for the **gentlemen** is the **left**.
The **Leading** foot for the **ladies** is the **right**.

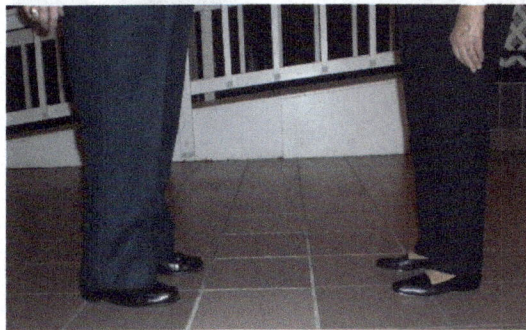

Count 1 - **Leading** foot slides forward toward your partner.

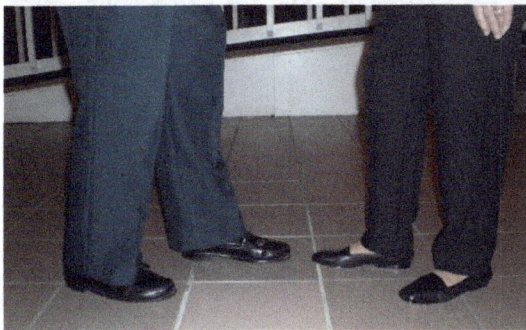

Count 2 - **Other** foot slides forward to join the **Leading** foot (feet are now together.)

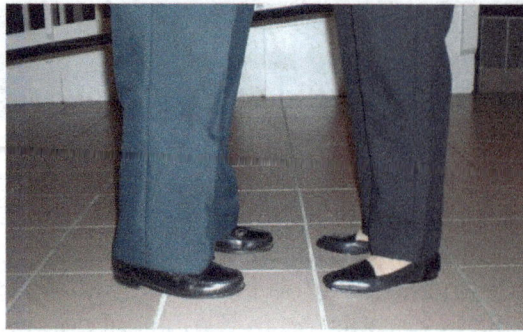

Count 3 – **Leading** foot slides back away from your partner.

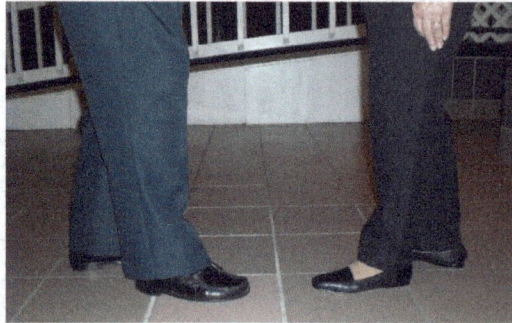

Count 4 - **Other** foot slides back to join the **Leading** foot (feet are now together.)

Count 5 - **Leading** foot steps in place (going nowhere.)*

Count 6 - **Other** foot steps in place (going nowhere) *

*Dancers stepping on the balls of their feet is called "sugar" so counts 5,6 will be "Sugar steps"

Style notes:
Bending the knees allows for sliding more smoothly. On counts 5,6 knees should bend even more.

Leading Notes for the Gentlemen:

   In the Shag, the hand that is holding your partner's hand never reaches out to the side, as it does in other swing dances. It collapses between the partners. At this early point in the lessons, the Gentlemen can lift their hands slightly and bring their elbows forward to touch their partner's elbows during every basic on Count 2. This creates the right space dynamic in the slot for the Gentleman to control, and the right amount of tension in both partners' arms. The arm will be lowered later in the lesson.

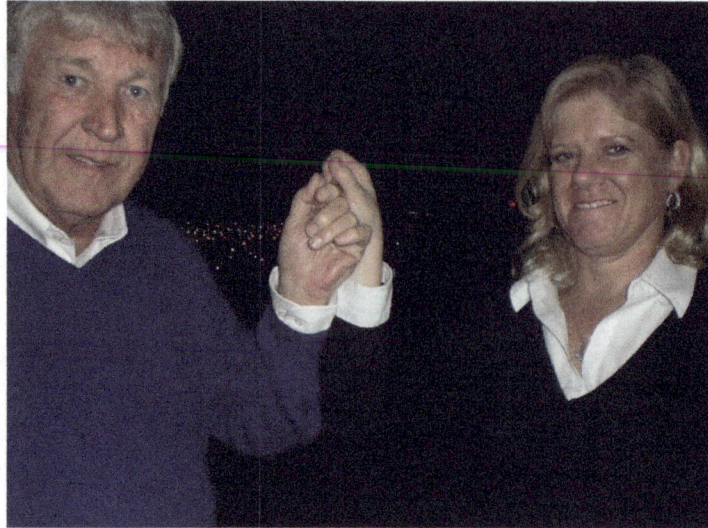

Another note for the Gentleman:

In order to find the downbeat and the tempo, Gentlemen should bend their knees (and Ladies follow) 3 times (6 musical counts) before beginning the first basic. In this way, the lady will be able to start on the beat with her partner without either person speaking.

In this Basic, counts 1 2 3 4 are the same as the Walking basic.
On counts 5 6, however, instead of Sugar steps in place, we will replace those 2 steps with "Ball Change".
This Ball Change is called "Rock Step" by most Shaggers.

Ball Change means to step on the **Ball** of the foot (see picture) on one beat and then **Change** the weight back to the other foot on the next beat.
In the Rock Step of this Shag basic, the Ball of the **Leading** foot is placed slightly behind the other foot.

Ball Change (Rock Step)
Count 5 – shift weight to the ball of the **Leading** foot in back.
Count 6 – shift weight back to the **Other** foot in front.

Walking Basic with Ball Change (Rock Step)
Count 1 - slide **Leading** foot forward toward partner

Count 2 -slide **Other** foot forward toward partner

Count 3 - slide **Leading** foot back away from partner

Count 4 - slide **Other** foot back away from partner

Count 5 – step on ball of **Leading** foot, placing it slightly behind **Other** foot

Count 6 – step on **Other** foot in place
(Counts 5, 6 are the Ball Change, also called the Rock step)

The Triple basic is the most common Shag basic. In Shag, there are variations on where the feet are placed in a triple step.

Rather than sliding single steps forward and backward as in the Walking basic, this basic utilizes a sliding triple step forward and back
This Triple step is similar to a "gallop" or "chaise" with one foot chasing the other in three movements. In the Triple step, the three steps are executed in 2 beats. Unlike a gallop, the Shag triple step is smooth, sliding on the floor with the dancers' knees bent, body weight on the balls of the dancers' feet, during the triple. This Shag Triple step slides forward and back within the same slotted space toward and away from your partner. It does not travel far because it is very small. In Shag, the dancers' feet sometimes do not even leave the floor.

*Now the Gentleman and Lady should hold only one hand, the Gentleman's Left and Lady's Right.

Triple Basic with Ball Change
To begin, separate feet, with **Leading** foot slightly in front of **Other** foot
The upbeat will be utilized in the Triple basic, so the counts will now be
 1-AND-2, 3-AND-4, 5 6.

Count 1 – slide **Leading** foot forward

Count AND — slide **Other** foot forward to the side of **Leading** foot

Count 2 – slide **Leading** foot forward
(**Other** foot is behind the **Leading** foot)

Count 3 – slide **Other** foot back
Count AND — slide **Leading** foot back to the side of the **Other** foot
Count 4 — slide **Other** foot back
(**Leading** foot is in front of the **Other** foot)

Count 5 – Ball (**Leading** foot)
Count 6 - Change (**Other** foot)

*Now that the student has learned three of the many Carolina Shag basics, the first improvisational choice is which to use as a personal favorite.
Choose one and let that be the basic used most of the time. The other basics will be used later as steps. Individuals do NOT have to choose the same basic as their partners. All Shag basics are on 6 musical counts and work together. Dancers who use different Shag basics are able to dance with each other instantly without any practice!

In Social Dance, the Gentleman leads. When the Gentleman prepares to turn the Lady, he has to "Set Up" the turn.
The Set Up is the hint to the Lady that something is about to happen.
Lady's turns, or any new step, happen at the beginning of a basic, on Count 1.
Since the Set Up must happen before the new step begins, the Set Up needs to happen at the end of the previous basic, on Count 6 (which in the Shag is the count before Count 1).

Reverse Turns

In these two turns, dancers will move past each other, changing places and ending up where their partner started. The footwork of the turn is the similar to the footwork as the individual's chosen basic.

Reverse Outside Turn

Count 6 – Set Up – as he finishes his basic, the Gentleman raises his Left arm, still holding his partner's hand, to make a bridge on his left.

Counts 1 AND 2 – the Gentleman takes his right hand, places it on the Lady's shoulder, and guides her under his bridge and past him as he moves forward past her, keeping her to his left. Partners are now shoulder to shoulder.

Counts 3 AND 4 - the Gentleman uses the footwork in his basic to turn to face the Lady, and since he is holding her hand, she will curve as well to face him using her footwork.

Counts 5, 6 – as the Gentleman and Lady complete the footwork in their chosen basics by executing their sugar steps or ball change/rock step, they are now facing each other and have changed places.

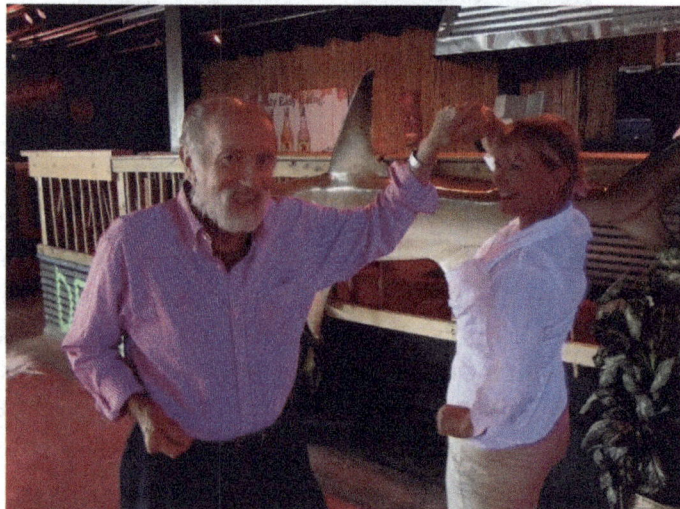

Count 6 – Set Up – as he finishes his basic, the Gentleman raises his Left arm, still holding his partner's hand, and moves their arms to his right so that the Lady's arm is across her face.

Counts 1 AND 2 – the Gentleman moves to the Left side of the Lady as she moves to Left side of the Gentleman. Partners are now shoulder to shoulder.

Counts 3 AND 4 – the Gentleman uses the footwork of his basic to turn to face the Lady, bringing his R foot forward to lead his second triple as he turns to his R. Since he is holding her hand, she will curve as well to face him using her footwork and utilizing a quick pivot on her R foot to her L on the "AND" before her second triple step which will go backward in her new direction facing her partner.

Counts 5, 6 – as the Gentleman and Lady complete the footwork in their chosen basics by executing their sugar steps or ball change/rock step, they are now facing each other and have changed places.

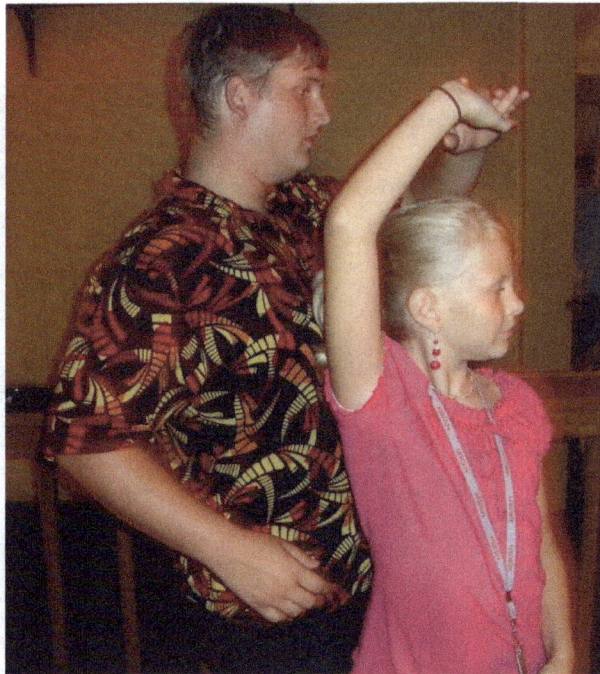

Leading/Following Notes: The Lady must wait for the Gentleman to set up the turn and then she must react instantly.
The Gentleman must remember to keep tension in his arm in order to guide the Lady, and to set up each turn properly as she does not know which one he intends. He must also loosen his hand grip so the Lady's hand can turn freely in

Dancers may rotate 360 degrees while they are doing the basic. The rotation is executed clockwise, and slowly. For example, dancers may execute 4-8 basics in order to make one rotation.

Rotating slowly means the dancers do not have to alter the basic as they move in the rotation. The Rotation is achieved by the Gentleman changing his angle slightly on Count 1.

The axis in the rotation is the couple's hands that they are holding.

***

Practicing Rotation will enable beginning dancers to learn the intermediate step, the "Pivot" more easily. It is helpful to know that on a crowded dance floor, dancers may not rotate and instead dance in their "slot" to make room for as many couples as possible. When room allows, however, dancers rotate and use steps such as the Pivot.

****

Young Shaggers at their first Jr. SOS festival.

Lesson 7
Improvisation- the Heart of the Shag

Improvisation means no planning. It means Just Do It!

In the Shag, each partner improvises steps by playing off what the other partner is doing. This takes lots of practice, not with one partner, but practice dancing constantly with many partners. Dancing consistently with only one partner will result in a decline in improvisational skills, so the best idea is to dance often with many partners.

The first aspect of improvisation for the beginning Shag dancer is deciding which basic to concentrate on, and once a favorite basic is chosen using the other basics as steps to insert occasionally keeps the footwork interesting and fun.

Unique to the Shag is the fact that partners do not have to be doing the same basic! As long as the basic that they are doing is executed on 6 musical counts, and partners are moving in the slotted pattern together, they can each choose their own basic variations and improvisations, with the Gentleman leading and the Lady following.

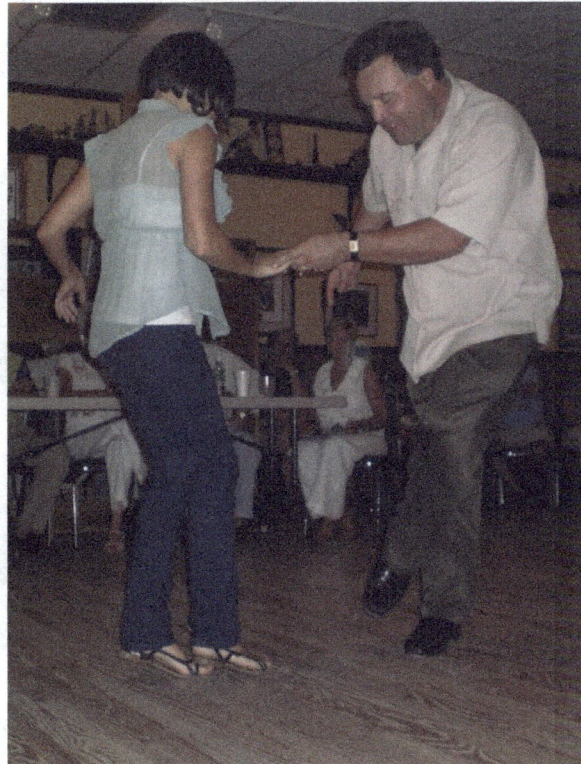

The next aspect of improvisation is for the Gentleman to choose when to lead a turn. The Lady must pay attention to his arm movement and react to his lead, improvising her footwork within his lead.

At this point, the student is becoming more proficient with leading and following, and the joined hands may be lowered to the more correct position at waist level, if not lowered already.

Shaggers hold only one hand, the Gentleman's Left and the Lady's Right hand. The Gentleman will still collapse his arm and control the space as he and his partner move toward each other on the first 2 counts, but he will keep it at waist level, without the partners' elbows touching anymore. The other arm stays by the dancer's side.

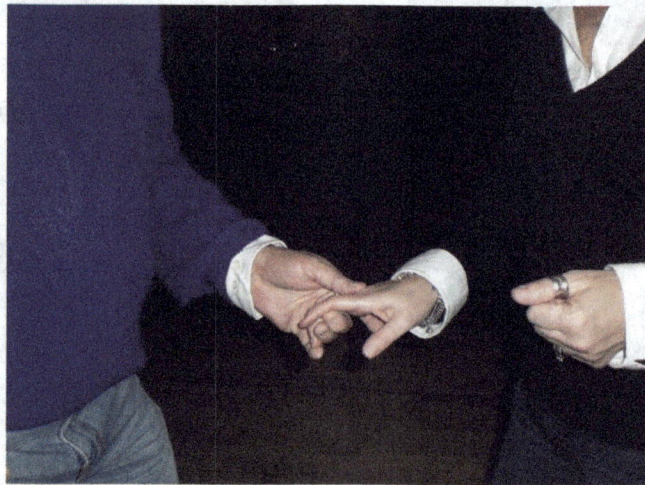

Now that the student has a main basic, two other basics to use as variations, two turns and a rotation, it is time to get on the dance floor and enjoy Shagging!

****

The Touch Basic, unlike the previous basics learned, is not a "constant weight shift" step. In dance, "Step" means to put one's entire weight on that foot, using the other foot next. "Touch" means to only put a toe or ball of the foot on the floor with no weight on it, preparing to use that foot again next.

Touch Basic

The count on this basic will be 1,2,3 AND 4, 5,6

Count 1 – **Leading** foot slides forward
Count 2 – **Other** foot slides forward with no weight, and rests with no weight on the ball of that foot beside the leading foot

Count 3 – **Other** foot slides back (beginning a triple step)
Count AND – **Leading** foot slides back chasing the Other foot
Count 4 – **Other** foot slides back (completing the triple step)

Count 5 – Ball (leading foot)
Count 6 – Change (other foot)

*This basic can be used as a continuing basic or as a step to insert during improvisation and is also widely used as the beginning step when Shaggers start their dance in the popular side-by-side position.

The Starting Position

The starting position for the Shag places the partners side by side, the Gentleman's right arm around the Lady's waist and the Lady's left hand on the Gentleman's shoulder, with the Gentleman holding the Lady's right hand with his left in front of the couple.

This is the way a couple begins the dance. The footwork of the Touch Basic is used. The partners complete one Touch Basic side by side and then on the next basic the Gentleman swings the Lady out so that she is in front of him, using that entire basic to accomplish this. Partners should be facing each other by Counts 5,6 of that basic. The second basic used to swing the Lady out may be the touch basic or the chosen basic of the individual. From this point on, the dancers are Shagging in the slotted position.

Remember, the spirit of the Carolina Shag is social dance, dancing with many partners, learning new steps, meeting people, and having fun! Introduce yourself, and dance with as many people as possible. The heart of the Carolina Shag lies not just in its technique or style, which has regional and generational variations, but in the dance's unique improvisational aspects. It is not a ballroom dance...in fact, it is a genre of its own.

"Good Friends, Good Times, Good Memories"
Jr. SOS— the Next Generation"

Dance/Shag Term Glossary

BALL CHANGE - step on, or slide onto the Ball of one foot, putting all the weight on that Ball, and then a Change of the weight back to the other foot, ending on that foot; Executed in 2 musical beats or less.

BASIC – refers to the step that defines a given dance by structuring the count and spatial dynamic; the step that is repeated over and over as the anchor for all other steps in that dance genre

BOOGIE WALK – Shag dance descendent of Shorty George, incorporating Rubber Knees and a lateral roll of the foot. May be executed forward or backward.

DRAG – movement of the foot on the floor without leaving the floor, traveling backward or sideways, not weight-bearing

DUCK WALK – Shag dance descendant of riff walks (tap dance).

HESITATION – an intentional pause in movement during the dance; dancer/s are usually motionless for 1 or 2 beats only.

IMPROVISATION – Just do it! No planning, instant reactions.
In Shag, it means partners playing off each other's movements as the gentleman leads.

INSIDE SUGAR WALK – executed with knees turned in

INSIDE TURN – the direction of the turn is in opposition with the leading foot; first step will be crossed to begin the turn

KINESTHETIC – learning in the muscles and body rather than the brain; muscles have memory.

OUTSIDE SUGAR WALK – executed with knees turned out

OUTSIDE TURN – the direction of the turn is the same as the leading foot; first step will be open to begin the turn

PIVOT – partial turn of the body with weight on the ball of one foot. In Shag, used to describe a fast rotation, similar to a ballroom "spot turn" but with footwork added.

PROGRESSION – a series of lessons beginning at a simple level, designed to build skills using the prior lesson/s as a base to work from.

ROCK STEP – In Shag, a small, smooth ball change in 2 musical beats that is part of a Shag basic, sometimes just a weight shift rather than having the feet leave the floor.

ROTATE – the slow turning of a person or two connected partners on their axis to any degree within a 360 degree space.

RUBBER KNEES – knees moving fluidly either in opposition or concordance, appearing to be made of rubber! A common Rubberknees move is executing sugar steps on counts 5,6 while knees beat together on counts 5,6!

SHORTY GEORGE – inside Sugar walk with Rubber knees, changing level from tall to short.

SLIDE – movement of the foot on the floor without leaving the floor, traveling forward, backward or sideways; may be weight-bearing or not

SLOTTED – Space used by partners in Shag and also in the Charleston, which indicates movements of each partner toward and away from the other in opposition forward and backward, rather than sideways.

SPIN – a very fast, balanced turn 360 degrees or more on the ball/s of the feet or foot; may be controlled or not.

STEP - weight shift onto one foot or ball of foot, all weight bearing, the other foot free

STYLE – the manner in which the movement is executed; movement quality

SUGARS – a family of dance steps incorporating a twisting pivot or steps on the balls of the feet.

SUGAR WALKS – sugar action (see above) while walking forward or backward on balls of feet

SUZI Q – a family of dance steps in which toes and heels move separately, either in opposition or concordance.

TECHNIQUE – the mechanics of movement, technical skills

TRIPLE STEP - 3 small steps or slides in 2 musical beats or less; a small smooth gallop or chaisse', one foot chasing the other, in 2 musical beats

TURN –the controlled rotation of one person either in one spot or traveling, a full 360 degrees or more; usually on the ball/s of the feet or foot.

VARIATION – a slightly altered version of a dance step or movement; may be given its own name or just referred to as a Variation.

WALK - a series of Steps, constant weight shift

WALKING BASIC – a basic that has a constant weight shift, all steps being taken on the downbeat

Musical Terms

BEAT – denotes the downbeat, which remains constant, counted in numbers

COUNT – monitoring dance movement, rhythm, and tempo by assigning musical beats a number. This is part of music theory which has been internationally universal for over 500 years.

RHYTHM –a combination of beats arranged in variations on a theme; the tie that binds music and dance together.

TEMPO – speed of the music, and therefore the dance.

TIME – a fraction in which one number denotes how many beats are in a measure and the other number denotes how many beats are assigned to the quarter note.

UPBEAT – the beat between the downbeats, counted by the word "AND"

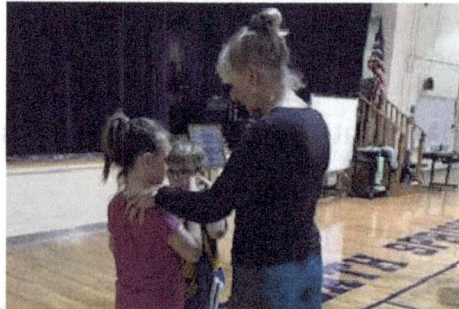

70

Shag Dance Information

The lessons in this book are simply an introduction to Shag dance.
To experience more steps and various styles, contact your local Shag club.

www.shagdance.com has links to Shag clubs, dance halls, SOS, Shag contests and events.

Many books have been written about Carolina Shag Dance history and culture, from each writer's unique perspective and memory.

Contact this author for information about Carolina Shag dancing, culture, or history at misscusa@gmail.com

Student Testimonials:

"I really like the Shag. The part I liked the most is the music. I liked it because the beat was cool." -Dakota, 3rd grader, Spartanburg County, SC

"I always wanted to know how to do the Shag. I like the rock step." –Mariana, 3rd grader Spartanburg County, SC

"I had fun learning Shag. It is better than recess!" -Asya, 3rd grader Barnwell County, SC

"I think I am going to use these steps when I grow up." –Edwin, 5th grader, Horry County, SC

"In Shag, people twirl and gentlemen lead. They have good music for Shag." –Jeremy, 3rd grader, Beaufort County, SC

"I liked Shag dancing a lot. Social dance means people are interested in other people and I can dance with anybody." –Corinthian, 3rd grader, Beaufort County, SC

"I didn't think I would like dancing with girls but it turns out I do like it." –Steven, 5th grader, Horry County SC

"She told us to take turns, and we had to hold out our hands, it was separate hands for the girls and the boys. It was fun; it was actually my first time learning to shag. We had talked about it in social studies, our teacher told us about it. It's the state dance because of the beach and the beach music. I'm going to keep on shag dancing when it gets hot, on the beach. This will help me know what to do when I go to a prom. I'll already know and be polite when I do it. I like to do all the moves, Ms. Hoadley taught us three parts- up together and back with six steps, the set up, and the turn. " – Deonte, 3rd grader in the Lowcountry Arts Integration Project, Beaufort County, SC.

Acknowledgments

Thanks To

Musical consultant Elizabeth Thode Hoard
(Juilliard (Institute of Musical Art) 1927, Juilliard graduate
diploma 1940, B.S. and M.A. Columbia University, Founder of
Bron School of Music.
Kristin Cambron, photo layout artist
The Lowcountry Arts Integration Project at Whale Branch
Middle & Elementary Schools, and
St. Helena Elementary School, Beaufort County, SC

Photo credits: M.A. Mueller, Lisa Annelouise Rentz, Otis Paris,
David Bogan, Tommy Howard,
Mark Judy, Caroline Hoadley, and
Monty Lee Photography

Special Thanks To

The Famous Feet of

Phil and Chick Sawyer, Loretta and Sam McIntosh,
Betty Kennedy Kane, Bubber Snow, Jeannie and Billy Pack,
And Jo-Jo Putnam

Shag dance and Beach music lovers

Sam and Lisa West, Charlie Womble, Jackie McGee, Ellen Taylor,
Pug Wallace, Cindy Simmons,
H. Lee Brown, the OD Pavilion, Rachel Stephens,
David Shaw & Duck's, Fat Harolds, and
SOS President Ron Whisenant.

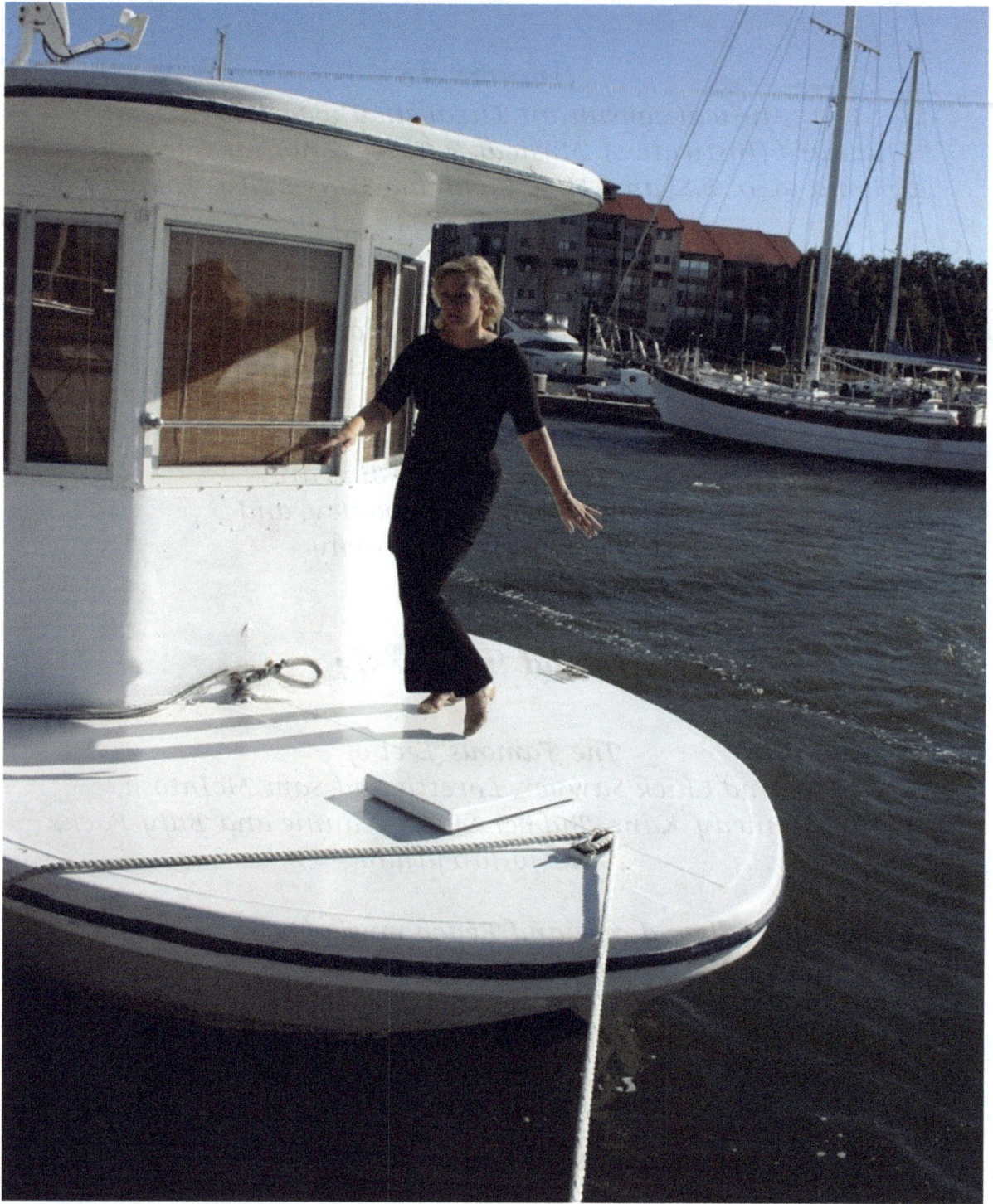

Caroline E. Hoadley is a choreographer, performer, and dance teacher for over 40 years. Director of the professional dance troupe The Moving Company, she is a former studio owner, a certified Life Member of Dance Educators of America, a state-certified K-12 dance education specialist providing master classes and standards-based residencies through the SC Arts Commission's Directory, a Kennedy Center-trained Teaching Artist, and a lifelong Shagger, as well as a 2023 inductee to Living Legends of Beach.

When not dancing on her mountaintop in Oconee County, SC, or the deck of her sailboat on the Carolina Coast, she is teaching dance or writing about dance and other subjects as she heads for the nearest dance floor at every opportunity.

*"If I knew then what I know now...I would have
never left this place..."*

ACT
OLD
LATER

Ocean Drive Pavilion Church

Sunday Mornings in the OD Pavilion

Church Service at 9:00AM

"Come As You Are,
Leave As You Should Be!"

Made in the USA
Monee, IL
13 June 2025